BELOW ARE THE SURVEY STATEMENTS

1. I have a consuming passion (*strong* desire, *great* concern) to reach people who don't know Christ.

2. I put *great* importance (high priority) on repentance (sorrow, regret, resulting in turning from sin).

3. I believe I am very discerning (perceptive) of other people's motives.

4. When I speak, I desire to stir other people's consciences (make them think, convict them to act).

5. I have an *unusually strong* desire to study God's Word.

6. I place *great* importance (value) on education.

7. When I do something, I like to see tangible results for my efforts, such as a finished project or measurable progress.

8. If I were to teach a group, I would prefer to deal with topics rather than verse-by-verse studies.

9. I am willing to assume a long-term personal responsibility for the spiritual welfare of a *group* of believers.

10. I am people-centered; I need many relationships.

11. I am *usually* soft-spoken.

12. I am patient, not one to jump into things, but am willing to respond to others' needs *quickly.*

13. I am fulfilled by performing routine tasks in the church for God's glory.

14. I am usually involved in or drawn to a variety of activities that help other people.

15. I keep my personal and business affairs well organized.

16. I have a burden (heartfelt desire, passion, great concern) to support missions.

17. I make decisions based strictly on facts and data.

18. I can clearly communicate goals in a way that others can fulfill them.

19. I believe salvation is the greatest gift of all, and am driven to tell others about this gift.

20. Some people think my witnessing methods are pushy.

21. I can spot (discern, point out, recognize) sin when other people cannot.

22. I have a desire to tell people about their sin.

23. I like to use visuals and books to support me when I teach or speak to a group of people.

24. I *constantly* search for better ways to do and say things.

25. I believe I am a very practical, pragmatic person.

26. I am able to provide helpful solutions and advice to others when they have personal problems.

27. I spend a *great* amount of time praying for other people.

4

28. I enjoy looking after the spiritual welfare of others; I am protective.

29. I find it easy to express my feelings to others.

30. I have a real burden (heartfelt desire, passion) to comfort others.

31. I am more fulfilled when I work behind the scenes, out of the public eye.

32. I am burdened (greatly concerned) with the physical and tangible needs of others.

33. My giving is a private matter between God and me.

34. I am sensitive to other people's financial and material needs.

35. I am goal-oriented, as opposed to being people-oriented.

36. I work best in a fast-paced environment, under pressure.

37. I have a desire to meet people who don't know Christ, even when they are total strangers, so I can share the Gospel with them.

38. I would rather witness (verbally share the Gospel, give my testimony) than do anything else.

39. I am grieved (bothered, troubled, disturbed, upset) with the wrong actions of others.

40. I am disorganized and must depend on others to keep me on schedule.

41. I have an organized system to store facts and figures.

42. I put more emphasis on the content of material than on people or the task.

43. I am more interested in studying the practical areas of Scripture that I can immediately apply to my life.

44. I put *great* importance on God's will.

45. I have a burden (compelling desire) to see others learn and grow.

46. I am more relationship-oriented than task-oriented.

47. I am very sympathetic and sensitive of others. I can "put myself in their shoes."

48. Other people think I am weak—a pushover—because of my lack of firmness.

49. I enjoy working with my hands.

50. I *often* let people talk me into doing things I do not want to do.

51. I am always ready and willing to give if a valid (real, proven) need exists.

52. I have the ability to *quickly* make wise decisions concerning finances.

53. I do things promptly; I make decisions quickly.

54. I dream big dreams and have great hopes, although I do not always share them with others.

55. I have a clear understanding of the Gospel and can relate it easily so others understand it.

56. I am socially active and always get along well with others.

57. I must verbalize (speak) my message; I would never be content to only write it.

58. I always express urgency and want others to make quick decisions.

59. Sometimes I would rather just write, but feel that I "must teach" because others would not present my message correctly.

60. The use of a verse out of context upsets me.

61. I develop several steps of action to solve every problem.

62. I question the value of deep doctrinal and theological studies.

63. I am very protective of people under my care.

64. Teaching the same material over and over would be boring and unappealing to me.

65. I attempt to show love and concern in all I do.

66. I act on emotions rather than just logic.

67. I am impressed and motivated when exhorted (encouraged) to serve.

68. I like to meet needs immediately (quickly).

69. When giving, I always like my gift to be high quality.

70. Other people misunderstand and think I am materialistic because of the importance I place on money. Much good can be accomplished through using money wisely.

71. I delegate whenever and wherever possible, but I know when and where I cannot.

72. I am willing to attempt impossible tasks for God.

73. I *greatly* rejoice in seeing people come to Christ.

74. I believe leading people to Christ (presenting the Gospel to non-Christians) is the greatest responsibility given to every Christian.

75. I enjoy speaking in public, and do it with boldness.

76. I am burdened (have a *strong* desire/conviction, am moved) to memorize Scripture.

77. I tend to question the knowledge of those who teach me.

78. Others accuse me of giving too many details.

79. I have the ability to motivate others.

80. Impractical teaching upsets and frustrates me.

81. I desire to give direction (guidance, instruction) to those under my care.

82. I am willing to study whatever is necessary in order to feed (nurture, guide) those for whom I care.

83. My heart goes out to the poor, the aged, the ill, the underprivileged, etc.

84. People who are hurting or excited seem to want to share their feelings with me.

85. I am already helping people while others are just talking about what to do.

86. I am quick to recognize and respond when other people need help.

87. I want to know my financial gift is being used properly; I believe in accountability.

88. I tend to judge others' success by the amount of their material assets.

89. I want to be a winner; I cannot bear defeat.

90. I am capable of making quick decisions and sticking to them.

91. When I share the Gospel or present my testimony to a non-Christian I always press for a decision.

92. Others think I am more interested in the number of people led to the Lord than in people themselves.

93. You must "prove" me wrong before I will go along with you.

94. Studying is too time-consuming; I rely on others to do my background work for me.

95. I prefer to develop my own material for teaching; other teachers' material would be hard to present.

96. I place great emphasis on word pronunciation.

97. Other people think I am not evangelistic because of my emphasis (focus) on personal growth.

98. I am accused of not using enough Scripture when teaching.

99. I enjoy doing a wide variety of activities rather than being confined to only one.

100. I perceive myself as a shepherd (an overseer, guiding and ministering to those under my care).

101. I am an emotional person; I tend to show my feelings and cry easily.

102. I identify emotionally and mentally with others. I am able to empathize (feel *with* others rather than just *for* others).

103. Some people think I neglect spiritual needs because of my focus on physical and practical needs.

104. I enjoy routine or hands-on jobs in the church.

105. I believe strongly that people should give financially according to their ability, and I tend to measure their spiritual growth on whether or not they do.

106. I am able to designate large sums of money for specific causes, and am not overly concerned even if others think I am trying to control ministry projects through my giving.

107. When there is no leadership in a group, I will assume it.

108. I have the ability to organize and harmonize the people with whom I work.

**FOLLOW THE INSTRUCTIONS ON THE ANSWER SHEET
TO TAKE THE SURVEY, THEN READ ON TO DISCOVER
WHAT YOUR GIFTS MEAN
AND HOW TO USE THEM**

THE EVANGELIST:
PASSIONATELY LEADING OTHERS TO THE SAVING KNOWLEDGE OF CHRIST

The Greek word *Euangelistes* means to proclaim glad tidings, a messenger of good. It denotes a proclaimer of the Gospel. The Evangelist can either be a preacher who stands before a crowd, imploring them to be saved, or perhaps an individual sitting in a living room or on a plane, trying to persuade someone to accept Christ. As an Evangelist you have the Spirit-given capacity and desire to serve God by leading people who are beyond your natural sphere of influence to the saving knowledge of Jesus Christ. You are sometimes classified as the passionate "soul-winner" who seeks to lead people to Christ.

As an Evangelist you are probably outgoing and personable. You compliment even strangers and are not afraid to ask them questions about their lifestyle and background. This opens the door to talk about their relationship with Jesus Christ—something you love to do. Be careful not to be overbearing or you may push some people farther away from hearing the Gospel.

You have great joy in seeing people come to Christ and are often consumed with the desire to confront non-Christians with the Gospel. You urge other Christians to do the same by directly telling them they must lead people to Christ or by encouraging them with your most recent "witnessing" experience. You must be careful, however, not to belittle them or make them feel unspiritual because they do not have a burden for the lost like you do.

You probably have memorized Scripture so you are not caught "empty-handed" while witnessing. Rather than waiting for opportunities to present the Gospel, the Evangelist often makes opportunities. Since you will influence so many people, you must be careful to live in such a manner that you do not bring reproach upon your message.

If you are a new Christian, you may want to begin using your gift by introducing your friends to people you respect who already have a pasion for sharing Christ with others. Perhaps you could pair up with an experienced Evangelist to follow up on others and visit strangers for the purpose of reaching them for Christ.

If you are a more mature Christian with experience in evangelizing, take a new Christian "evangelist" under your wing. Share your experiences with him or her and provide encouragement. Continue to look for opportunities to share the Gospel and lead people to Christ.

Beware that Satan can attack your gift by causing you to take the credit and develop pride over the number of people you have led to Christ. This type of pride can also stunt your spiritual growth and ability to learn, and cause you to view others as numbers rather than people with needs. As well, when you tend to see people as numbers, it can lead to discouragement when converts are few or infrequent.

HOW CAN YOU USE THIS GIFT?

There are ways you can carry out the gift of Evangelism. Visitation programs are the most obvious. You may enjoy visiting juvenile detention centers or jails, going door-to-door, going to orphanages, shelters for women or the homeless, and of course, following up on visitors in their homes. Your gift is a plus for leading people to Christ during an invitation or altar call. You can participate in special evangelistic efforts, such as fairs and other events. Your gift also fits well in church planting, on Gospel teams, in migrant ministry, men's or women's conferences, and many public speaking ministries.

THE PROPHET:
BOLDLY AND FEARLESSLY PROCLAIMING GOD'S TRUTH

The Greek word *prophétes* means "a prophet, poet; a person gifted at expositing divine truth." This gift goes beyond the call to expose other people's sin and teach the truths of God's Word, to actually doing something in daily life to use the gift—to expose injustice and expound the truth, and to lead people to make changes that are biblically based. As the Prophet "tells forth" God's Word, knowing what God's Word teaches and expects of us, the Prophet also leads others to make a difference in today's society and world.

To be Prophet is to be a "forthteller," telling or "speaking forth" the mind of God: boldly preaching, speaking, and teaching God's Word. You are very discerning; one who points out sin with the goal of making people aware of sin in their lives so they will repent. A Prophet in full-time Christian service may be a preacher, often traveling to churches, evangelistic events, and on missions trips. You have the Spirit-given capacity and desire to serve God by proclaiming His truth.

As a Prophet you have an ability to see that which is wrong. In fact, you tend to easily spot what is wrong and have to look to find something right. You probably spend much time praying and even weeping over the sins of the Church and for those who have yet to accept Christ. You have a great burden for the sinful condition of the world around you. Because of this, you take every opportunity to proclaim that everyone must repent or perish.

You have a strong sense of duty and can sometimes be perceived as being opinionated, impatient, and likely more serious than lighthearted about life. You enjoy being alone, but would rather be in a group than relate to people one-on-one. You desire to speak publicly. You are able to make quick decisions and want things done right. You are likely hard-working, devoted, able to discern people's motives and character, and willing to stand up for what is right.

Other people may misinterpret your intensity as being overly demanding or insensitive toward people's feelings. One of your greatest challenges is to keep a spirit of love. Remember to "speak the truth in love" (Eph. 4:15) and not to be judgmental. If you keep a tender, loving heart, you will be a blessing in your home, church, and to individuals; you can make a real impact on their spirituality. Be careful to let the Holy Spirit convict people, rather than trying to convict them yourself. Work on being positive, patient, and tactful.

Beware of Satan's attack on your gift. He may try to cause a lack of compassion and forgiveness, bring discouragement because of unrepentant attitudes by others, entice you to fall into the very sins you speak against, or cause pride and self-righteousness over lack of certain sins.

HOW CAN YOU USE THIS GIFT?

There are several avenues in which to carry out the gift of Prophecy. Revival speaking is certainly a fitting ministry. You can pastor well if you have a secondary gift of Shepherd. You are a great help in problem-solving for a church with a sin problem. You could also serve in teaching on Gospel teams, in prison ministry, in migrant ministry, and in counseling to help bring awareness of sin in a person's life. You could speak at conferences and retreats. You would serve well as one who promotes causes you believe in, stands up for those who have been wronged, teaches God's Word, and provides counsel to others. Depending on your secondary most dominant gift and your abilities, you may serve as one who initiates action, plans events, leads an evangelism or missions team, acts as a mediator to get to the points and come up with a plan of action, counsels those who have fallen away and need help getting on track, helps raise funds and speaks for humanitarian organizations, or works as an advocate for children or victims of crimes, as a committee member for ministry planning, as a prayer and accountability partner, or as a Bible teacher.

THE TEACHER:
MAKING CLEAR THE TRUTH OF GOD'S WORD WITH SIMPLICITY & ACCURACY

The Greek word for teacher *didaskalos* means master, teacher or doctor. As a Teacher you are one who communicates knowledge, guides, makes known or relays facts. You are likely more in-depth than the average Sunday school teacher. You have the Spirit-given capacity and desire to serve God by making clear the truth of God's Word with accuracy.

As a Teacher you live to learn and teach (or perhaps write if you teach through the written medium). You should learn to teach in two manners which may be contrary to your nature: the material must be simple so students can understand it, and it must be practical. The Shepherd/pastor, the Prophet, and the Exhorter (those with speaking gifts) usually rely on your resources to help fulfill their responsibilities.

You love the Word, enjoy reading, may be a little shy of strangers, are creative and imaginative, and prefer teaching groups over individuals. You are generally confident, self-disciplined, and sometimes technical. You probably love charts, graphs, and lists. You would sometimes rather just do research, but "must teach" because others would not teach it the way you would. The use of a verse out of context upsets you and you question the knowledge of those who teach you. You are organized and enjoy studying. You are so concerned with accuracy that you often dwell on the trivial, giving others the feeling that you give too many details.

Be careful that you are not critical of people who differ with your doctrine and that you do not measure other people's spirituality by their amount of Bible knowledge. Be willing to listen as well as talk. Don't hesitate to read directions and work on developing tolerance for others' mistakes.

If you score high in the gift of Teaching and very low in the gift of Shepherding, you probably won't make a good Sunday school teacher or group leader. Your tendency will be to relay knowledge and not shepherd or minister to the other needs of your students. People who use the gift of Teaching in vocational service usually become teachers of teachers, professors, authors, or in-depth researchers.

Beware of Satan's attack on your gift, as he may try to cause pride and a feeling of superiority due to the knowledge you acquire. This can be reinforced when others consider you to be the "final authority" on certain subjects.

Also, resist the temptation to lose sight of people's needs, or place information above people. And if people don't seem to respond to your teaching, guard against discouragement and disenchantment creeping in, or killing your drive or zeal.

HOW CAN YOU USE THIS GIFT?

You do not necessarily have to teach the Bible to be a help to the church ministry. Although you can help with interpretation or teaching teachers and others, you may teach in areas such as education, business, finance, or computers. You may enjoy writing and developing curriculum. You would probably serve well as a Bible institute teacher or a correspondence course instructor. Your gift also lends itself to the mission field where you could serve as a missionary/teacher. You may want to teach a basic doctrine course to newcomers or new Christians or host quarterly small group studies on different topics. You may enjoy doing research for the pastor or others who teach.

THE EXHORTER:
MOTIVATING OTHERS TO ACTION, APPLICATION AND PURPOSE

The Greek word *parakaleo* means to admonish, to encourage, to beseech. You are a "how to" person. You have the Spirit-given capacity and desire to serve God by motivating others to action by urging them to pursue a course of conduct. In a teaching position, you are able to explain how to apply God's Word. Your goal is to present material that enables the Holy Spirit to promote change in the student's life. You reach out and help Christians become more mature.

As an Exhorter you are a very practical person, a good counselor, tolerant of others, serious-minded, orderly, and usually impulsive. You are expressive in a group setting; the group listens when you speak. You are comfortable working one-on-one or in groups. You are enthusiastic and talkative and enjoy encouraging others.

You are burdened to show how Scripture relates to conduct and have a desire to unify people by using practical rather than doctrinal issues. You likely place great importance on God's will and believe that His Word has the answer for every problem. You tend to make decisions logically rather than on feelings, and are very orderly.

Be careful not to interrupt other people; your enthusiasm sometimes makes you guilty of this. Others may think you don't use enough Scripture in teaching because you tend to use Scripture to support what you are teaching, rather than starting with Scripture.

Unlike Teachers, you have the willingness to teach the same material again and again, updating and perfecting it as you do. As a counselor you usually have the ability to leave other people's problems "in the office" rather than letting them drag you down.

Beware of Satan's attack on your gift. He may cause pride in your motivational abilities. He may influence you to lose sight of people because of program emphasis. Don't become discouraged when results are not evident. Be careful not to encourage others to do the wrong things through your persuasive abilities.

Many times we are convicted that we need to make changes in our lives but the problem is we just don't know how. We need practical steps in order to go forward. The one who provides such practical steps in a person's life is the Exhorter. Exhorters spend their time teaching people how to do things; they are application-oriented people. Exhorters have practical steps for everything. Unlike the Teacher that teaches chronologically, the Exhorter teaches topically; pulling Scriptures from throughout the Bible to support a single topic. They also motivate, encourage, and excite people, leading them to get more done. They make great counselors because they tend to provide practical solutions to problems.

HOW CAN YOU USE THIS GIFT?

You may use your special gift in many areas. You may want to be a leadership trainer. You could certainly serve as a counselor in church or in a counseling center. You could teach in church training or seminars or even small groups. You would make a good online or telephone ministry worker and would be a tremendous volunteer to follow up with new converts. You would work well as an encourager with those who are discouraged, and as a counselor in a drug or alcohol program, rescue mission, poverty program, half-way house, or in a shelter for abused women and children. You could also use your gift in organizing or serving in a men's or women's ministry.

THE SHEPHERD:
OVERSEEING, TRAINING, FEEDING, COACHING/LEADING

The Greek word *poimen* means pastor. Although the word *poimen* is translated pastor only one time in Scripture (i.e., in Paul's spiritual gifts listing in Ephesians 4:11), it is used sixteen additional times. The remaining sixteen are all translated "shepherd." Therefore, we are actually discussing the *gift* of Shepherding, not the *position* of pastor. Though a good pastor must have the gift of Shepherding, everyone who has the gift of Shepherding is not called to be a pastor. The gift can be used in many positions in a church.

As a gifted Shepherd, you have the Spirit-given capacity and desire to serve God by overseeing, training, and caring for the needs of a group of Christians. You are usually very patient, people-centered, and willing to spend time in prayer for others. You tend to be a "Jack of All and Master of *one*," meaning you are usually dominant in one of the speaking gifts (Evangelist, Prophet, Teacher, Exhorter) as well. You are often authoritative, more a leader than a follower, and expressive, composed, and sensitive. Your pleasing personality draws people to you.

You have a burden to see others learn and grow and are protective of those under your care. You want to present the whole Word of God and do not like to present the same materials more than once. You are willing to study what is necessary to feed your group and are more relationship-oriented than task-oriented. You are a peacemaker and diplomat—very tolerant of people's weaknesses. You tend to remember people's names and faces. You are more concerned with doing for others than others doing for you. You are faithful and devoted and may become a workaholic. You can become an all-purpose person in order to meet needs.

People with the gift of Shepherding make the best Sunday school teachers and group leaders because their desire is to go beyond just teaching or leading, to shepherd and minister to the daily needs of their students. The position of Sunday school teacher or group leader is an extension of the pastoral ministry in the church. These groups should be shepherded on a small scale, the same as the pastor shepherds the whole congregation on a large scale.

Be careful to involve other people; don't try to do it all yourself. Work on holding people accountable. Do not be overly protective of your "flock." Because of these potentially weak areas, other people may think it is your job to do all the work; they rely too heavily on you. You may be expected to be available at all times, know all the answers, and be at every function. Learn when to say no.

Beware of Satan's attack on your gift. He will cause discouragement when the load gets heavy, and pride because your "sheep" look up to you. You may develop family problems because of too little time and attention. You may become selfish when "sheep" feed in other pastures.

HOW CAN YOU USE THIS GIFT?

This gift is a great help in many areas. You may serve as a Sunday school teacher, small group leader, pastor or assistant pastor, special ministry leader (such as youth, children, men, etc.), nursery worker or as a half-way house or other type of shelter volunteer. You may consider serving as a dormitory leader in a college, orphanage, children's home, etc. Scout troops would appreciate your assistance as a den leader.

11

THE MERCY-SHOWER:
IDENTIFYING WITH AND COMFORTING THOSE IN NEED

The Greek word *ellos* means to feel sympathy with or for others. As a Mercy-Shower you have the Spirit-given capacity and desire to serve God by identifying with and comforting those who are in distress. You understand and comfort your fellow Christians. You enter into the grief or happiness of others and have the ability to show empathy which is to feel *with* others, not just *for* others.

As a Mercy-Shower you are willing to deal with and minister to people who have needs that most people feel very uncomfortable working with. You seem to say the right thing at the right time. Your personality is likely one of soft-spoken love. It hurts you to scold someone; you are very non-condemning. People love you because of all the love you give them. You find it easy to express yourself and are outgoing with a low-key, inoffensive personality. You are easy to talk to, responsive to people, a good listener, peaceable, and agreeable. You tend to make decisions based on feelings more than fact and like to think about things for a while before making a decision.

In your burden to comfort others, your heart goes out to the poor, the aged, the ill, the underprivileged, and so on. You tend to attract people who are hurting or rejoicing because you identify with them. Be careful not to let others use you. Try not to resent others who are not as understanding as you. Refrain from becoming a gossiper when you are around other Mercy-Showers. Do not let your circumstances control you. Because of your supernatural ability to show mercy, others accuse you of sticking up too much for people, being a softy and a compromiser. They may think you are too emotional.

Mercy-Showers make excellent counselors. Left untrained, however, you may destroy yourself by your tendency to take people's problems home with you. Your empathy can become detrimental without personal training on how to deal with it.

Beware of Satan's attack on your gift. He can cause pride because of your ability to relate to others. He may influence you to disregard rules and authority. You may experience a lack of discipline because of strong feelings for those who hurt due to disobedience and sin. Don't fall into Satan's trap of complaining and griping.

HOW CAN YOU USE THIS GIFT?

Harkening to Dickens' famous opening line in The Tale of Two Cities, *your gift is best used in both "the best of times . . . and the worst of times." In other words, God has gifted you to minister in times of sorrow and in times of great joy. It fits well with another gift of service such as deacon, youth worker or hospital visitation. With a counseling course, you could become a good counselor. You may serve as a hospital, nursing home, or shut-in worker; a funeral coordinator and provider of sympathy and support; or a poverty center worker. You would do well as an usher or greeter and welcome-center worker or hospitality person. You may want to work in a telephone ministry. You would make people feel welcome on a newcomer visitation team. Other appropriate ministry areas include missions, committee member, furlough assistance, and correspondence helper. You would work well with the elderly and with people who have mental and physical disabilities, in nursing, and with special ministries to migrants, released offenders or victims of abuse.*

THE SERVER:
PROVIDING PRACTICAL HELP BOTH PHYSICALLY AND SPIRITUALLY

The Greek word *diakonia* means to do service. In Acts 6:1 the word is interpreted "ministration." Our word deacon comes from the same Greek word. Actually the gift of Serving combines helps and ministering. The word "helps" is used in 1 Corinthians 12:28 and "ministering" in Romans 12:7. As a Server you have the Spirit-given capacity and desire to serve God by rendering practical help in both physical and spiritual matters. You enjoy meeting the practical needs of your fellow Christians and the church.

The gift of Serving is not the gift God gives you when you cannot do anything else. It is spiritual in nature and as important as any gift in the church. Never think it is anything less; it only becomes less if you do not use it as God intended.

As a Server you are the person who is willing to do a million and one necessary tasks in the church. You probably do not realize that your love for the Lord is showing every time the doors of the church are open, especially if you oiled the hinges last week so they don't squeak any more. You are happy working behind the scenes. You are ambitious, often involved in a variety of activities, and enjoy manual projects. You are loyal, sincere, tolerant, faithful, and devoted. Most people find you easy going, likable, congenial, and inoffensive. You can listen to others without being critical. You do not like to be in the spotlight and prefer not to express yourself publicly.

You are quick to respond to needs and impressed with the need to respond when exhorted to serve. Because of this, you find it difficult to say no. You like to support a good leader. Some consider you a workaholic. You tend to emphasize practical needs over spiritual needs.

Be careful that you complete what you start and do not neglect the needs of your own family by trying to meet so many needs in the church or in others' homes. Be willing to read and follow directions in the beginning—not just when all else fails. Because of your quick response, some people think you jump in too fast. Others think you neglect spiritual needs.

Beware of Satan's attack on your gift. He can cause pride because of the work you do. He may cause you to feel insignificant or cause you to lack concern for people or for spiritual growth. Impatience and lack of knowledge cause poor-quality workmanship.

HOW CAN YOU USE THIS GIFT?

Your gift may put you into action. You may serve as manager of maintenance and grounds. You can do may tasks such as paint the walls, pick up trash, sort hymnals, clean the baptistery, keep the nursery or launder nursery bedding, cook meals, paint signs, drive the bus, help with the choir, run errands, serve as an audio-video worker, help with recordkeeping, be the church librarian, act as a greeter or an usher, serve as a stage hand in drama productions or as a photographer. You may want to help in special ministries such as migrant or community help (with home repairs or meals-on-wheels for the needy and elderly), as a hospitality worker for newcomers, or as an instrumentalist. You may also enjoy beautifying the church grounds with flower gardens and landscaping. The list goes on.

THE GIVER:
RELEASING MATERIAL RESOURCES TO FURTHER THE WORK OF THE CHURCH

The Greek word *metadidomi* means to give over, to share, to give to, to impart. As a Giver you have the Spirit-given capacity and desire to serve God by giving of your material resources, far beyond tithing, to further the work of God. You have a strong desire to meet the financial needs of your fellow Christians and church members.

As a Giver you probably feel that the best way you can give of yourself is to give of your material gain for the work of God. You give without public recognition and usually do not want people to know who you are nor how much is given. You disapprove of anyone who gives for the wrong motives. Your motive is to further the work of God and meet real needs, not to show off or get something in return.

You are usually well organized, keep to yourself, have an accurate self-image, are interested in helping people, and are conscientious and self-disciplined. You may also have the ability to make money. You are sensitive to the financial and material needs of others, alert to needs others overlook, ready to give, want your gift to be high quality, make quick decisions concerning finances, want to ensure your gift is used properly, and may have a burden for missions.

Chances are your spouse also has the gift of Giving.

Be careful not to measure other Christians' spirituality by the amount of their giving, or their success by the amount of their material assets. Realize that though God has called everyone to give, He has not called everyone to give as you do. You are sometimes misunderstood as being materialistic because of your emphasis on money. Some people think you try to control them with your money, and may be jealous of you.

Beware of Satan's attack on your gift. He can cause pride because of the amount you give, blindness to spiritual needs and qualities and to other areas of service, and discontent when decisions are made contrary to your interests. Do not develop a critical attitude toward those who are not able to give. Make sure you have the right motives for giving and serving Christ. Don't mistake your burden for giving to missions as a call to the mission field. Don't neglect to give to the necessity of other Christians (as challenged in Romans 12:13) by giving only to church projects. Remember you can still give even if it is not tax deductible.

HOW CAN YOU USE THIS GIFT?

Your gift is welcome anywhere large or small amounts of money are needed. You can serve as a member of a finance or budget committee or a missions or building committee. You may make a good trustee. You would serve well as a member of a school board or commission. You would do great service as a poverty, rescue mission, or migrant mission committee member. You could sponsor or underwrite special projects, online, radio, or TV ministries. Always be aware and willing to meet needs of an individual apart from programs. In this sense, you could serve on a benevolence committee or give to support such a ministry. You may want to support a men's or women's ministry, a shelter for the temporarily unemployed and homeless or the abused, or contribute to children who do not have parents.